PETER BROOK

Peter Brook is one of the world's best-known theatre directors. Outstanding in a career full of remarkable achievements are his productions of *Titus Andronicus* (1955) with Laurence Olivier, *King Lear* (1962) with Paul Scofield, and *The Marat/Sade* (1964) and *A Midsummer Night's Dream* (1970), both for the Royal Shakespeare Company. Since moving to Paris and establishing the International Centre for Theatre Research in 1970 and the International Centre for Theatre Creation when he opened the Théâtre des Bouffes du Nord in 1974, he has produced a series of events which push at the boundaries of theatre, such as *Conference of the Birds* (1976), *The Iks* (1975), *The Mahabharata* (1985) and *The Tragedy of Carmen* (1981) to name but a few. His films include *Lord of the Flies* (1963), *King Lear* (1970), *The Mahabharata* (1989) *Tell Me Lies* (restored 2013) and *Meetings with Remarkable Men* (restored 2017). His hugely influential books, from *The Empty Space* (1968) to *The Quality of Mercy* (2013), have been published in many languages throughout the world.

MARIE-HÉLÈNE ESTIENNE

Marie-Hélène Estienne joined the Centre International de Créations Théâtrales (C.I.C.T.) in 1977. She was Peter Brook's assistant on *La Tragédie de Carmen*, *Le Mahabharata*, and collaborated to the staging of *The Tempest*, *Impressions de Pelléas*, *Woza Albert!* and *La Tragédie d'Hamlet* (2000). She co-authored *L'homme qui* and *Je suis un phénomène* performed at Théâtre des Bouffes du Nord. She wrote the French adaptation of Can Themba's play *Le Costume*, and *Sizwe Banzi est mort* by Athol Fugard, John Kani and Winston Ntshona. In 2003, she wrote the French and English adaptations of *Le Grand Inquisiteur* (*The Grand Inquisitor*) based on Dostoyevsky's *Brothers Karamazov*. She was the author of *Tierno Bokar* in 2005, and of the English adaptation of *Eleven and Twelve* by Amadou Hampâté Bâ in 2009. With Peter Brook, she co-directed *Fragments*, five short pieces by Beckett, and again with Peter Brook and composer Franck Krawczyk, she freely adapted Mozart and Schikaneder's *Die Zauberflöte* (*The Magic Flute*) into *Une flûte enchantée*. She co-created *The Suit* in 2012 and *The Valley of Astonishment* in 2013, both performed at the Young Vic, London.

BATTLEFIELD

from *The Mahabharata*
and Jean-Claude Carrière's play

directed and adapted by
Peter Brook and Marie-Hélène Estienne

NICK HERN BOOKS
London
www.nickhernbooks.co.uk

A Nick Hern Book

Battlefield first published in Great Britain in 2017 as a paperback original by Nick Hern Books Limited, The Glasshouse, 49a Goldhawk Road, London W12 8QP

Battlefield copyright © 2017 Peter Brook and Marie-Hélène Estienne

Peter Brook and Marie-Hélène Estienne have asserted their moral right to be identified as the authors of this work

Cover photograph of the original production of *Battlefield* (2015) by Simon Annand

Designed and typeset by Nick Hern Books, London
Printed in the UK by Mimeo Ltd, Huntingdon, Cambridge PE29 6XX

A CIP catalogue record for this book is available from the British Library

ISBN 978 1 84842 705 1

Introduction
Peter Brook and Marie-Hélène Estienne

The origin of theatre in every culture is always storytelling. Whether in the family, in the village, in the courtyard of the temple, it is one person sharing a story with one group of avid listeners.

When Peter Brook and I, with Jean-Claude Carrière, went to India to prepare our nine-hour stage adaptation of *The Mahabharata*, we experienced directly how this vast, rich and complex epic had lived over a thousand of years through an unbroken chain of narrators.

Today, as always, the storyteller needs no more than a simple stick to bring to life armies, rivers, Heaven.

Gradually, over the centuries, this has developed through many other forms: dance, mime, song. To try, for an outsider, to imitate these forms is pretentious and often useless.

Now, feeling the need to bring the epic into today's world where its questions are so passionately alive, we felt that the ending had to be explored in a different manner from the way it had been explored thirty years before. The question of how to reign when a terrible war is finished, leaving on the ground millions of corpses, when there are no more fathers, children, friends, allies, when they are all dead – how can the future king accept his mission, which is to be king? How can the old, blind king, his uncle, accept the situation, having lost his hundred sons, and all his warriors, teachers, generals? Where is

Dharma, the divine law, the reason why the text has been written, to maintain its power on human beings, even if they forgot it?

With a small group of actors, putting their art at the service of the whole and with a musician using one unique instrument, we started our journey, from the battlefield to an unknown silence.

July 2017

Battlefield, based on *The Mahabharata* and Jean-Claude
Carrière's play, was first produced at Théâtre des Bouffes
du Nord, Paris, on 15 September 2015, with the following
cast:

Carole Karemera
Jared McNeill
Ery Nzaramba
Sean O'Callaghan
And the musician Toshi Tsuchitori

Adapters and Directors	Peter Brook and
	Marie-Hélène Estienne
Music	Toshi Tsuchitori
Lighting	Philippe Vialatte
Costumes	Oria Puppo
General and Light Manager	Philippe Vialatte
Stage Manager	Thomas Becelewski

It was a production of C.I.C.T. – Théâtre des Bouffes du
Nord, Paris, in a co-production with the Young Vic
Theatre, London; Les Théâtres de la Ville de
Luxembourg; PARCO Co. Ltd, Tokyo; Grotowski
Institute, Wrocław; Singapore Repertory Theatre; Théâtre
de Liège; C.I.R.T. (Centre International de Recherche
Théâtrale); Attiki Cultural Society; and Le Cercle des
Partenaires des Bouffes du Nord.

The production received its British premiere at the Young
Vic Theatre, London, on 3 February 2016.

Characters

KING DRITARASHTRA, *Father of the Kauravas*
VIDURA, *brother of Dritarashtra*
YUDISHTIRA, *their nephew*
KUNTI, *mother of Yudishtira*
KRISHNA
BISHMA, *grandfather of Yudishtira*
GAUTAMI
HUNTER
SNAKE
DEATH
TIME
MAGNIFICENT KING
PIGEON
FALCON
RISHI
WORM
GANGA
NARRATOR
MONGOOSE
MARKANDEYA
BOY

And a MUSICIAN

Note on Text

The story unfolds in a very simple space, with a minimum of accessories. The little group of actors is like one story teller. One after the other, like with a single voice, they evoke both place and time.

A blind man comes in, he is DRITARASHTRA, *the king, followed by his brother* VIDURA. *They walk on the battlefield, it is the end of the war between members of the same family, cousins fighting cousins, the Kauravas and the Pandavas.*

DRITARASHTRA. The war is over. The war is over. My eldest son Duryodhana is dead. My hundred sons are dead, all their children are dead! All their armies, their battalions, their generals are dead.

To hell with the state of humanity! To hell with the human body! All the woes that we suffer in this life arise from the very state of humanity!

How can I go on? I am condemned to wander without eyes over this ravaged earth and the only sound I hear is the sound of the teeth of carnivorous creatures devouring corpses.

Where is Justice?

VIDURA. Dritarashtra, your sorrow causes your limbs to burn and your wisdom is destroyed. With that sorrow you even regard death as preferable to life.

You now have to take your son's enemy, the victor of this war, your nephew Yudishtira, in your arms. You have to help him reign on this kingdom which was once yours.

As for me, now that the war is over, I have to follow my path, I have to leave you and spend my last days in the woods!

DRITARASHTRA. You helped me day after day during that terrible battle – without you, how can I live?

VIDURA. Dharma, Justice, the law, Dharma will help you –

— — —

We are now on another part of the battlefield. In this endless space, YUDISHTIRA, *the winner of the war, contemplates in despair the bodies of millions of warriors covering the earth.*

YUDISHTIRA. The sun is slowly rising over the battlefield covered by endless heaps of corpses.

This victory is a defeat. What have we done?

The golden breastplates and the jewels of the heroes glitter in the sun. The earth is covered by their lances, their bows, their arrows, their clubs and the sharp steel of their swords.

Some of the warriors are standing upright, glued together, some are glued to the earth.

The battlefield is invaded by blood-hungry creatures. Birds of prey and vultures, dripping with blood, seize dead feet, tear them apart, and devour them by the millions. These invincible warriors, annihilated, are now the prey of herons, cranes, eagles, vultures, jackals, dogs.

Who could have ever foreseen such massive destruction?

These tiger-like men are now extinguished fires. They were lying in soft beds, and now they lie on the earth, only softened by their blood.

Hear the vultures' and the jackals' cries, only caught by the deaf ears of the dead.

These sinister and cruel enemies invade the battlefield with their insatiable appetite. Sometimes the vampires do not dare touch bodies that are still intact – they think, 'These ones are still alive!'

The women arrive. Devoured by grief, they sadly surround these heroes. Their faces shine, covered by tears. They lament, wandering in all directions, striking themselves violently.

The earth is covered by heads, hands, limbs, all twisted together in great heaps. Seeing that terrible sight they go out of their minds. In their madness after putting a head on a corpse, without seeing another one nearby, they shout – 'It's not his!'

Fighting off the vampires, they put together arms, thighs, feet. Even when they see their husbands, they do not recognise them.

Another task is waiting for me. I must do what has to be done.

— — —

YUDISHTIRA. Let the oblations be made for our dead. Let our priests burn them and throw their ashes into the River Ganga. Let our women pray for their families.

Let them cry and shout their despair loud – let the earth
listen to that sad complaint – let her be happy – she
won – there are no more warriors disturbing her peace
on the battlefield –

— — —

In the distance appears KUNTI, *the mother of*
YUDISHTIRA. *She calls her son.*

KUNTI. Yudishtira!

YUDISHTIRA. Yes, Mother? What is it?

KUNTI. There is still another person left.

YUDISHTIRA. One person left?

KUNTI. Yes. You have to do the oblation for him also,
my son.

YUDISHTIRA. I do not understand, I remember all our
dead only too well, surely I am not so ungrateful as to
forget who died for me. Who is this person to whom an
oblation from me is due?

KUNTI. It is Karna, you must make the oblation for him
too.

YUDISHTIRA. Karna? But, Mother, why should I do it for
Karna? He was not one of us, his father is a charioteer,
the funeral rites must be performed by him. Why do you
ask me to do it for that man who was our arch-enemy?
Why should I do it, Mother? Please tell me.

KUNTI. My son, you must do it because Karna was of
noble birth.

YUDISHTIRA. Of noble birth! Mother, you know nothing about Karna. How do you know that he was of noble birth? Then you must know who he was. Why should I offer the funeral oblations for him? Who was his father? Tell me, Mother, who was he?

KUNTI. His father was Surya, the sun. Karna's mother was a young girl. She was given a mantra, she could call a god at her will, she used it one night, it was like a game for her – but to her great surprise when she asked the sun to come, he came. She tried to resist him but he told her that he could not come down from the sky for nothing. He gave her a beautiful child.

She was afraid of the censure of the world. So she had to keep the secret buried in her heart. She placed the child in a wooden box and set it afloat on this same river – this Ganga. The child was taken up by a charioteer, he gave him to his wife, and they named him Karna. He loved his name, he would not take any other name. His real mother was a princess, she did this injustice to her first-born, she has several children but her heart is empty because of this.

YUDISHTIRA. Mother, who is the mother of Karna? Who is that woman who was so heartless that she could abandon her child in the River Ganga the moment he was born? Who is the woman who ruined the life of that great man? You must know, since you are telling me the details of the crime. Who is she, Mother?

KUNTI. That woman is still alive. I am that woman. Karna was my son, my first-born.

YUDISHTIRA. When I heard that he was dead I ran to the battlefield to see if he was really dead. I was so happy to see him dead. It was an immense relief,

I thought, 'At last, I've won!' I even cried out, 'Now I am the king!'

Did Karna know that he was my brother? Did he know who he was?

KUNTI. Yes. I went to see him before the war, I asked him to come to you, but he would not. He would not let down his friends. It was against his nature to be disloyal to his king, master and friend, your cousin Duryodhana. He suffered agonies when he knew he was your brother. Knowing who he was, he let you win.

What are you doing?

YUDISHTIRA. I'm going into the woods.

KUNTI. Do you intend to give up your kingdom?

YUDISHTIRA. Yes. I'll go into the woods. I will eat fruits and roots, I will wash twice a day, without tears, without joy, like an idiot, calm in the face, deaf and blind, wandering aimlessly, seeking neither death nor life.

KUNTI. Don't go, my son. I'm begging you. Remember – before the war, you asked Krishna –

— — —

Suddenly, KRISHNA *appears.*

YUDISHTIRA. What can save the world?

KRISHNA. You. You are the only one. The earth needs a king who will be calm and just. I want this king. Without him, I am lost.

YUDISHTIRA. Am I this king?

KRISHNA. Yes. Destruction never approaches weapon in hand. It comes slyly, on tiptoe, making you see bad in good and good in bad. Anyway, you won't have the choice between peace and war.

YUDISHTIRA. What will be my choice then?

KRISHNA. Between a war and another war.

YUDISHTIRA. The other war – where will it take place? On a battlefield or in my heart?

KRISHNA. I don't see a real difference.

KRISHNA *vanishes*.

KUNTI. The earth will need you. She will enjoy your victory. She will need you to wake up again, to recover her beauty, her harmony, her calm.

— — —

The blind king, DRITARASHTRA, *approaches*.

DRITARASHTRA. Where is Yudishtira? Lead me to him –

YUDISHTIRA. Yudishtira, fit to be cursed, kneels before you –

DRITARASHTRA. I am the one who must be cursed, the guilt is mine. My heart must have been made of stone not to explode as I was told, day after day, the details of this terrible massacre. I listened to no one, to none of the voices that told me – 'Stop this hatred, hold back the greed of your son!' – I was mad not to listen.

My son was cruel, his egoism was insatiable, it had no limits. He had only one word on his lips – 'war' – but I loved him, that love had no limits, I followed his madness. And now every one of our children has been destroyed.

This morning I could not see any other way than to die. But now I see clearly, even without my eyes, that my duty is the reverse. Despite this terrible battle I did not bear you any hatred but only love, I must take you in my arms, you are now my son and as your father I must help you in your duty to become the king that everyone awaits –

YUDISHTIRA. No, Father – This kingdom is yours. You are the king.

DRITARASHTRA. My dear son, I told you before the war that your victory would burn you day and night, for you will have destroyed your family – you have to be king – you cannot escape your destiny. You know that there is still one man alive on the battlefield who could convince you. Bishma, your grandfather. He is lying on a bed of arrows that pierce his body. He is waiting for the day of his death that can only arise when the solstice returns.

When you were a child you wanted so much to learn from him. In his mind he is calling you, go to him. He'll help you.

KUNTI. Yes, my son, go to him.

— — —

We are now on another part of the battlefield, where
BISHMA, *the ancestor of both families, the invincible*
warrior who can decide the moment of his death, is lying
on a bed of arrows. YUDISHTIRA *joins him.*

BISHMA. I heard that your understanding is clouded by
the many doubts you have –

YUDISHTIRA. How can my understanding not be
clouded, when I am the cause of your dying,
Grandfather? I fought against you. Millions and
millions of men have perished on my account, I cannot
find any peace of mind. I believe Brahma created man
to do evil.

BISHMA. What makes you think, Yudishtira, that the
Creator is responsible for all a man does? Above all,
for his crimes? We must see things as they are. The
Creator is not implicated in actions, and for he who
knows this, all bad actions cease. He who knows this
knows that it is his nature that acts and acts in
obedience to the laws of great Nature.

— — —

The stories are immediately brought to life by the actors,
playing all the roles.

GAUTAMI. One day, Gautami, who is possessed of great
patience and peace of mind, finds her son dead. A
hunter arrives with a snake carefully tied up.

HUNTER. Madam, this snake killed your son. Shall I
cut it now into little pieces, or should I throw it into
the fire?

GAUTAMI. Let him go. Killing him won't bring back my son. Free him, don't do him any harm.

HUNTER. Madam, you seem to know the difference between right and wrong, and your noble soul is touched by the suffering of any creature. But I haven't a noble soul, I'm just a practical man and I'm going to kill this snake – give me your leave to do so.

GAUTAMI. It was my son's destiny to die so I can't authorise you to kill the snake. Be merciful, forgive him and let him go.

HUNTER. An enemy deserves to die. Killing an enemy brings one merit. In this life, as well as the next.

GAUTAMI. Pardon brings even more merit.

HUNTER. This snake is a killer, if I kill this snake, thousands of lives will be saved.

GAUTAMI. But not my son.

SNAKE. Senseless hunter, what have I done! I'm only a snake! I've no free will, I've not committed any crime. Yama, the Goddess of Death, sent me to do what I did. If you have to blame somebody, blame her!

HUNTER. Maybe, but you accepted to do it, you're the instrument of the crime. The potter's wheel is the unique cause of the pot's existence and you are the reason this child died. You are guilty, you admit it – so you have to die.

SNAKE. The potter's wheel is not the only cause of the making of a pot, and I'm not entirely the cause of the death of the child. Two causes – or even more – can operate together. I'm not guilty of any crime. My guilt results from interlinked causes.

HUNTER. I don't know the difference between a primary cause or an interlinked one – but I know well that your bite killed the child. You must die. Do you think that when a crime is committed its author is not responsible? Tell me what you think of this.

SNAKE. Primary cause or not, nothing happens without a cause somewhere on the way, and you're right, I am that somewhere-on-the-way cause, but I think the real culprit is the one who incited me, Yama, Death.

HUNTER. You talk too much –

DEATH. At this precise moment, Death itself arrives.

What are you talking about? I am Yama – Death. More than everyone I have no free will. If you have to blame somebody, blame the real responsible one – Time.

HUNTER. Wait. If Time is the guilty one and not you, Death – why do we spend all our life trying to ignore you, or is Time responsible for that as well?

TIME. At this point, suddenly, Time appears.

Neither the snake, nor Death, and not even me, Time, with all my power, are responsible for the death of that child.

It is Destiny who is responsible. Destiny. Destiny leads us all.

GAUTAMI. Let the snake be free. I told you from the start it was Destiny which was the cause of my son's death.

— — —

BISHMA. So you see, Yudishtira, Destiny governs us all. What happened on the battlefield was not your fault nor that of your enemies. The earth called on Destiny to exterminate all these heroes. She suffered too long from being trampled on by arrogant men and you had to serve Her.

YUDISHTIRA. Was it just? Was the earth's demand just? What is it to be just? How can one be truly just?

BISHMA. Yudishtira, you are the son of Dharma – and Dharma is Justice, the law. He is in the heart of all creatures. But so often he is not heard. Being born like that, you always want to be just, to be sure it is just to be just! You are always searching for the truth, and not being satisfied by easy answers or lies, and so unhappy when you have to lie, so you go on and on with your search. It is not easy to be born tempted by justice. It is rare and sometimes it is even very painful.

Once, a falcon spent many long hours chasing a splendid pigeon. The pigeon, with great difficulty, quivering with fear, managed to reach a magnificent king and settled on his knees.

— — —

KING. Why are you trembling? You are completely safe here. Don't be afraid. Your feathers are so beautiful, they have the colour of the first buds of the blue lotus, and your eyes the tender rose of a pomegranate. Here you should have no fear. If need be, I'll give up my kingdom to save you.

FALCON. This pigeon is mine. It belongs to me, I chased him so he's mine. I'm dying with thirst, I'm famished, I'm desperate. Give me my pigeon. Your duty is to take care of your subjects. You can't deprive a poor starving falcon. Your power extends to your enemies, your servants, your subjects, but you have no authority over the creatures of the sky.

KING. Prepare a bull, a boar, a buffalo, and two pigs, and give them to this falcon. Let them satisfy his hunger. As for the pigeon, he will stay with me.

FALCON. I don't like buffalo's meat, and even less pig's, it is against my religion. My food is pigeon. But if you're so attached to this bird, give me instead a piece of your thigh – that's exactly the same weight as the pigeon.

KING. Granted.

BISHMA. A pair of scales is brought and a well-sharpened knife. The pigeon, trembling, is put on one of the scales. The king takes the knife and cuts off a large slice of his flesh and puts it on the other scale. But the scales remain tilted towards the pigeon. The weight of the pigeon far exceeds the weight of the king's flesh.

The king chops off another piece and throws it onto the scales, and then another, and another, but the weight of the pigeon still exceeds the weight of the king's flesh.

The king cuts off all his flesh, and in the end when he is no more than a skeleton, he climbs onto the scale, but the weight of the pigeon still exceeds his weight. Then, to his amazement, the two birds jump on his shoulders and tell him –

PIGEON *and* FALCON. We have heard that you were a very just king, we were sent here to test you, and now we know that really you are just.

BISHMA. And together they vanish into the sky.

— — —

BISHMA. So you see, Yudishtira, justice is the duty of a king, and its price can be very, very high.

YUDISHTIRA. All those heroes who gave their life in the great battle, what will happen to them? It is not easy to give up one's life, even on a battlefield. Tell me, O Bishma, you who know everything.

BISHMA. In the meanders of life, Death is always there.

Listen, I will tell you a story that I never told you before.

— — —

BISHMA. One day, a Rishi walking on a highway used by chariots, saw a worm trying to get to the other side, as quickly as he could.

RISHI. Why are you in such a hurry, worm? What are you afraid of?

WORM. Of a chariot, Sir, I hear it coming, it's going to crush me. I must get to the side, I can hear the crack of the whip. Life is precious, I have no intention of dying if I can avoid it. I don't want to lose this paradise of life for the hell of death.

RISHI. But you are only a worm, what do you know
about the paradise of life? The joys of sound, smell,
taste, touch have no meaning for you – You'd be much
better dead.

WORM. You see, Sir, despite all you tell me, I like my
life. I'm used to it, I love it. And even if I am only a
worm, I have my pleasures. In a previous life I was
very rich, I had a very bad character, I was cruel and
vulgar, I cheated many of my friends, the prosperity of
others drove me mad, I hated their fortunes, their
houses, their beautiful wives. But I did love my mother,
and it happened to me to give shelter to a holy man.
And when I got old, like a father who has lost his son,
I repented. Obviously that didn't work so well, but
I am sure that one day, if I deserve it, I shall obtain
liberation.

RISHI. Wait, listen.

A man is walking in a dark, dangerous forest, filled
with wild beasts, the forest is surrounded by a vast net,
he is afraid, he runs to escape from the animals, he falls
into a pitch-black hole. By a miracle, he is caught in
some twisted roots. He feels the hot breath of an
enormous snake, its jaws wide open, lying at the
bottom of the pit. He is about to fall into these jaws. On
the edge of the hole, a huge elephant is about to crush
him. Black-and-white mice gnaw the roots from which
the man is hanging. Dangerous bees fly over the hole
letting fall drops of honey. Then the man holds out his
finger – slowly, cautiously – he holds out his finger to
catch the drops of honey. Threatened by so many
dangers, with hardly a breath between him and so many
deaths, he still can't throw off his chains. The thought
of honey holds him to life.

Deprived of his senses, in that wilderness, he never
loses at any time the hope of prolonging his life.

WORM. That man was in a terrible situation, I
understand, so with the greatest respect I must leave
you.You see I really want to stay in this world and if it
is my destiny to die under the wheel of a chariot, well,
this time I must try and avoid it.

RISHI. He was not quick enough, he disappeared under the
wheel of the chariot. Where is he now? Nobody knows.

— — —

BISHMA. This world is ever threatened by Death. The
nights which come and go do but lessen the span of
one's life. Death waits for no man. It is nearing every
creature every moment. Its progress is imperceptible,
but it is ever steady. With each passing day, man's life
is shortened. Death comes before man's desires have
been fulfilled. Death snatches a man away like a beast
of prey carrying away a ram. What you have planned to
do in the afternoon must be done at dawn. Death is
ruthless. Life is so uncertain and only death is certain,
it may come now or it may come years later. The
readiness is the most important.

Man is plagued by a thousand desires, his work, his
lands, his children, his home, all these have woven a
web of attachment from which he is torn away by
death. Nothing can resist this web of attachment except
Truth. Truth is immortality. In the same body can be
found the germs of death as well as immortality. It is all
in your hands if you nurture the one or the other.

Truth is the duty of every human being. It is an eternal duty. Truth is the highest refuge. Truth is the greatest penance. Truth is immutable, eternal, unchangeable.

The sun is approaching its solstice. Yudishtira, the hour of my death has come.

— — —

DRITARASHTRA *and* KUNTI *join* YUDISHTIRA.

BISHMA. Dritarashtra, my son. You know all the duties of a king, there is nothing that you do not know. Wise as you are, you should not grieve for the death of your sons. It was Fate. Even if you cannot see it, a light has been saved.

Kunti, my daughter, forget your sorrow. Your first-born, Karna, loved you. He understood you. Do not grieve.

Yudishtira, Grandson, don't despise yourself. You are the most upright, you are the truest of men. It needed this harsh battle within yourself, your doubts, and this terrible war, for you to become the king that the city awaits.

Grant me leave. I will now cast off my body.

— — —

YUDISHTIRA *stays alone with* BISHMA *as he leaves his body.*

YUDISHTIRA. Bishma's face is lit up by an unearthly smile. He closes his eyes and lays still for a few moments. He holds back his life breaths and wills himself to die. Then the life breaths of Bishma, piercing through the crown of his head, shoot into the sky. They rise up and become lost in the clouds. A cool breeze blows, the earth breathes again. A strange peace fills the heart of men as the soul of Bishma goes on its journey.

The ever-present Krishna, who has suddenly appeared, says –

KRISHNA. Excellent, excellent!

YUDISHTIRA. A great funeral pyre is built, and the body of Bishma is cremated. His bones and ashes are brought to the banks of his mother, the River Ganga. Suddenly, the waters stop, the river opens, and Ganga herself appears.

— — —

A woman in despair, GANGA, *rises from the ground.*

GANGA. Yudishtira! Listen to me! My son could not be killed unless he accepted it. He wanted you to be the king everyone awaits. You will reign for thirty-six years, and after these thirty-six years, a new era will come and you will have to let your kingdom to your grandson – the only child who has been saved from this great battle. You will go to the high mountains and there you will find the peace you're looking for.

Now let my sorrow be heard.

KRISHNA. Do not yield. Be comforted. Return to your
river.

YUDISHTIRA. She re-enters the water, and the river
flows peacefully once more.

— — —

We are now in YUDISHTIRA*'s palace.*

NARRATOR. Yudishtira is crowned king and he performs
an extraordinary sacrifice. According to the laws of
kings, he distributes all his riches to the priests.

And then a small animal enters, a mongoose, half-
covered with gold. She throws herself into what is left
from the great sacrificial fire.

YUDISHTIRA. What are you doing, mongoose?

MONGOOSE. I'm trying to use this melting gold to cover
the other part of my body, but it's not working. Your
sacrifice, according to the law of kings, is not right.
You're giving all your riches to the priests who don't
need it. You should be giving it to the poor.

YUDISHTIRA. You're right. What should I do then?

MONGOOSE. Well… Perhaps you should change the
law! But the real sacrifice is in the heart, not in the laws.

YUDISHTIRA. You're right, mongoose. Give all that
gold to the poor.

Mongoose, the real sacrifice must be in the heart, but I
will change the law.

— — —

Still in YUDISHTIRA*'s palace, after many years.*

NARRATOR. Many years passed under King Yudishtira's reign. And the people were very happy.

Dritarashtra was treated with the utmost respect. Yudishtira tried all the time to make him happy. He issued no orders except with his approval. In the administration of the affairs of the state, he always consulted him and conducted himself so as to give him the feeling that, in truth, the kingdom was ruled by him.

Fifteen years had passed when, one day, Yudishtira discovered that his uncle was fasting and sleeping on the ground.

— — —

YUDISHTIRA. I did not know. I did not know that you've been fasting and sleeping on the bare ground, mortifying your flesh in this manner. I believed that you were well looked after and happy!

DRITARASHTRA. My son, it is time for me to go into the woods – I can no longer stay under your roof. You treated me as your father, you offered me everything you could offer. But my heart desires silence. As my king, give me permission to go into the woods.

YUDISHTIRA. You ask for my permission to go. How can I give or refuse permission to you? Do not desert me.

KUNTI *takes her son by the arm, they walk together.*

KUNTI. My son, do what Dritarashtra desires! Let him go to the forest. Let not Dritarashtra die here! Do not stand in the way of his wish. Let him go and live among the honeyland flowers of the forest.

The Dharma of kings is to die in battle, or spend their last days in the forest. You are too young for that.

The time has come for him, my son, and for me, too, the time has come.

I must go and live in the forest, smearing my body with filth, engaged in the performance of penance. Do not try to make me change my mind. I am firm.

YUDISHTIRA. Strange indeed is this purpose of yours. I ask you not to accomplish it, I can never give you that permission. It is your duty to show me some compassion.

You wish to abandon me to the kingdom?

KUNTI. I do not desire the fruits of that sovereignty which has been won by you. I wish to attain, by penance, peace in my heart.

YUDISHTIRA. How will you live in the inaccessible woods?

KUNTI. I desire to waste my body through penance. My son, let your understanding be always devoted to righteousness. Let my mind be free.

YUDISHTIRA. So be it, Mother!

NARRATOR. The next morning, Dritarashtra, followed by Kunti, left for the forest, mourned by all the city.

— — —

KUNTI *and* DRITARASHTRA *have reached the forest.
They are sitting on the ground.*

NARRATOR. One day, Yudishtira decided to go to the
forest. He reached the place where his mother and
uncle were fasting. They were very happy to see him.
They offered him roots and fruits.

YUDISHTIRA. Does your peace, your self-restraint, your
tranquility of heart grow? Is my mother able to serve
you without fatigue and trouble? Will, O King, her
residence in these woods be productive of fruits? I
hope you no longer give way to grief for your children,
all of whom, devoted to their duties, have been slain on
the field of battle. Do you still accuse me, who is
responsible for their slaughter?

DRITARASHTRA. My dear son, all that is in the past.
There is no more grief in my heart.

VIDURA (*calling from far away*). Yudishtira! Yudishtira!

YUDISHTIRA. That is the voice of Vidura, my
beloved uncle. He is calling me. I know that after the
war he came here – you must know where he is –

DRITARASHTRA. My dearest brother Vidura is
mortifying himself and is living on just air. He is in the
heart of the forest and does not come here any more. If
you go deep into the woods, you will find him.

— — —

YUDISHTIRA *finds* VIDURA *in the depth of the forest.*

YUDISHTIRA. I went towards Vidura. He was not the
old Vidura I knew – his body was a bundle of bones
and he was almost dying. But his eyes were glowing
with a strange intensity. I went to him, I said – 'I am
Yudishtira, my lord. Speak to me.' He stood, leaning
against a tree. I found myself compelled to look
straight into his eyes. His eyes burned into mine.
Our four eyes were locked for a while. I couldn't
withdraw my eyes from his eyes. A strange thing
happened. I felt myself stronger and wiser. I felt
different. I felt I was more Vidura than myself.
I realised that he was dead and that he had entered my
body and had abandoned his.

— — —

YUDISHTIRA *comes back to the place where*
DRITARASHTRA *is sitting.*

YUDISHTIRA. Vidura has died. I wanted his body to be
cremated, and then I heard his voice telling me, 'No, do
not cremate my body, for it is part of you now.' I feel
an inexpressible gratitude. I've always wanted to go
into the woods, but I must serve the destiny which has
been given to me. I will go back to the city.

KUNTI. Yes, my son, you must leave, you must go back
to the city. If you stayed there, we would not be able to
achieve our penances.

DRITARASHTRA. My dear son, you are right, go back to
your duty. Let us die in peace.

— — —

KUNTI *and* DRITARASHTRA *are wandering in the*
forest when, suddenly, DRITARASHTRA *has a vision.*

DRITARASHTRA. I see a whole army rising out of the
    river. All my sons, their wounds healed, reconciled, an
    immense wave of men, all white, mounting into the air.

KUNTI. I see my son, Karna, he's coming towards me,
    he's smiling, he is in front of me, he takes me by the
    hand, he leads me to the river, he enters into it, and he
    disappears.

DRITARASHTRA. I had eyes. I could see my sons! I
    could see my sons for the first time. I saw them
    disappear into the river. Now I cannot see anything any
    more.

    Kunti, I always knew that Karna was your son.

— — —

Some time later, the NARRATOR *comes in with*
YUDISHTIRA *and tells him what happened to his mother*
and uncle.

NARRATOR. Yudishtira, listen with calm, as I tell you
    what happened after you left the forest. The old king
    and your mother wandered from a place to another.
    One day when they were near the River Ganga, a wind
    rose high and a fierce forest fire began to consume the
    forest. All the animals came to the river and jumped
    into it – snakes, boars, tigers – and when the forest was

afflicted on all sides and such distress came to all the creatures, it was clear that Death was approaching.

And your mother told Dritarashtra –

— — —

We are now in the forest with the elders.

KUNTI. There is a fire in the forest

DRITARASHTRA. Yes, I can feel the smoke

KUNTI. It's easier than I thought

DRITARASHTRA. Cross the river, save your life

KUNTI. I feel the fire's breath

DRITARASHTRA. Cross the river, save your life

KUNTI. Come with us. Put your hand on my shoulder. Let us both walk towards the flames.

— — —

YUDISHTIRA *is alone in his palace.*

YUDISHTIRA. Eighteen years had passed, after the death of the elders, when Yudishtira starts to see in the heavens the same omens that were seen just before the great battle.

Fathers and mothers slay their children. Girls of six and seven give birth. Boys of eight become fathers.

Trees, dry and barren, are bereft of fruits and flowers.
Wild animals invade the cities.

Winds, dry and strong, showering gravel and stones,
blow from every side.

Birds wheel, making circles from right to left.

Rivers run in opposite directions.

The horizon is always covered with fog. Meteors fall
on the earth.

When they rise, the rays of the sun are blocked by
trunks of headless men.

Circles of light are seen every day around the moon
and the sun. These circles have three hues: Black.
Ashen. Blood-red.

— — —

Suddenly, MARKANDEYA, *the ascetic, who was once
the last living being on the devastated earth, appears.*

YUDISHTIRA. Markandeya, is it true that this world will
be destroyed?

MARKANDEYA. It has happened already – and it will
happen again. And again. And again.

When neither the sun nor the moon nor fire nor earth
nor air nor sky remained, when all the world, being
destroyed, looked like one vast ocean, I alone
remained.

I wandered over that grey, misty swamp and my heart
became dry. I could not find any living creature nor any

place where to rest. After months and months of
wandering in the waters, one day, suddenly, I saw a
vast banian tree, and sitting at its foot I saw a boy.
Wonder filled my heart. I asked myself – 'How does
this boy sit here alone when the world itself has been
destroyed?' And although I have knowledge of the
Past, Present and Future, I failed to understand who he
was and why he was sitting there, and he said to me
with a smile –

BOY. O Markandeya, I see that you cannot find rest, come
into my body.

MARKANDEYA. He opened his mouth and I dropped
into his belly. In the stomach of that boy I saw rivers,
mountains, oceans. I saw people, cities, kingdoms. I
saw the firmament, the sun, the moon, planets, stars,
galaxies. In the belly of that child, I saw everything.

After years and years of travelling in that belly I never
found its limits. I was ravaged with anguish as I could
not understand the real meaning of it all, and I could
not find any rest. I called the boy for help – and at once
I was ejected out of his mouth.

Then I found myself sitting right next to him, he
gratified me with a big smile and said –

BOY. Markandeya, you are too impatient. Having dwelt
for so little time in my body, you did not find the rest
that you were looking for! Come closer. Listen.

Now I will tell you who I am and all you wish to
know –

The MUSICIAN *plays on his djembe, and all the*
actors listen.

The End.